The Stinking Rose

Sujata Bhatt was born in Ahmedabad, India in 1956, and spent her early years in Pune. She has lived, studied and worked in the United States, and is a graduate of the Writers' Workshop at the University of Iowa. In 1992 she was the Lansdowne Visiting Writer at the University of Victoria, B.C., Canada. She currently lives in Bremen with her husband, the German writer Michael Augustin, and their daughter. Sujata Bhatt works as a freelance writer and has translated Gujarati poetry into English for the *Penguin Anthology of Contemporary Indian Women Poets*. She received a Cholmondeley Award in 1991. Carcanet publish her first two books of poems: *Brunizem* (1988) received the Commonwealth Poetry Prize (Asia) and the Alice Hunt Bartlett Award; *Monkey Shadows* (1991) received a Poetry Book Society Recommendation.

Also by Sujata Bhatt from Carcanet

Brunizem
Monkey Shadows

SUJATA BHATT

The Stinking Rose

with illustrations by
ROLF WIENBECK

CARCANET

First published in 1995 by
Carcanet Press Limited
402–406 Corn Exchange Buildings
Manchester M4 3BY

A CIP catalogue record of this book
is available from the British Library
ISBN 1 85754 048 4

The publisher acknowledges financial assistance
from the Arts Council of England

Set in 10pt Palatino by XL Publishing Services, Nairn
Printed and bound in England by SRP Ltd, Exeter

Funded by
THE
ARTS
COUNCIL
OF ENGLAND

For Michael and Jenny Mira
as always

Acknowledgements

Thanks are due to the editors of the following publications in which some of these poems, sometimes in different versions, first appeared: *New Statesman & Society, PN Review, Poetry Review, Poetry International 1992, Tandem* (UK); *Poetry Ireland, The Cuírt Journal* (Ireland); *The Malahat Review, Rungh* (Canada).

Some of these poems have appeared or will appear in the following anthologies: *One for Jimmy* ed. Matthew Sweeney, Hereford and Worcester County Council, 1992; *Into the Nineties: Post-Colonial Women's Writing* ed. Shirley Chew and Anna Rutherford, Dangaroo Press, 1994; *Leave to Stay* ed. Joan Riley and Briar Wood, forthcoming.

A number of poems were broadcast on *Kaleidoscope*, BBC Radio 4. The free translation of Marina Tsevetayeva's poem, *Ophelia in Defence of the Queen*, was commissioned by the South Bank Centre for *Poetry International 1992*. *Nothing is Black, Really Nothing* was commissioned by the Arts Council of Great Britain and the South Bank Centre for *Out of the Margins: African, South Asian and Caribbean Writers in Britain*. A group of poems (now rearranged in this volume) originally appeared in a chapbook/pamphlet entitled *Freak Waves*, published for the Hawthorne Society by Reference West, Victoria, BC, Canada, 1992.

Special thanks are due to the Creative Writing Department of the University of Victoria (in Victoria, BC, Canada) for the Lansdowne Fellowship and to the *Senator für Kultur und Ausländerintegration* in Bremen for a grant which provided much assistance towards the completion of this book.

Special thanks also to Rolf Wienbeck for sharing ideas and paintings on the garlic theme, and to Jürgen Dierking for translating some of these poems into German.

I am very grateful to Eleanor Wilner and Michael Schmidt for their helpful comments.

Contents

IV Old World Blood

V રિયાઝ (Riyaj)

I
Freak Waves

The One Who Goes Away

There are always, in each of us,
these two: the one who stays,
the one who goes away –

Eleanor Wilner

But I am the one
who always goes away.

The first time was the most –
was the most
            silent.
I did not speak,
did not answer
those who stood waving
with the soft noise
of saris flapping in the wind.

To help the journey
coconuts were flung
from Juhu beach
into the Arabian Sea –
But I saw beggars jump in
after those coconuts – a good catch
for dinner. And in the end
who gets the true luck
from those sacrificed coconuts?

I am the one
who always goes away.

Sometimes I'm asked if
I were searching for a place
that can keep my soul
from wandering
a place where I can stay
without wanting to leave.

Who knows.

3

Maybe the joy lies
in always being able to leave –

But I never left home.
I carried it away
with me – here in my darkness
in myself. If I go back, retrace my steps
I will not find
that first home anywhere outside
in that mother-land place.

We weren't allowed
            to take much
but I managed to hide
my home behind my heart.

Look at the deserted beach
now it's dusk – no sun
to turn the waves gold,
no moon to catch
the waves in silver mesh –

Look
at the in-between darkness
when the sea is unmasked
she's no beauty queen.
Now the wind stops
beating around the bush –

While the earth calls
and the hearth calls
come back, come back –

I am the one
who always goes away.

Because I must –

with my home intact
        but always changing
so the windows don't match
the doors anymore – the colours
clash in the garden –
And the ocean lives in the bedroom.

I am the one
who always goes
away with my home
which can only stay inside
in my blood – my home which does not fit
        with any geography.

We are Adrift

At night
our sunroom is closer
to the water –
we are adrift with the moon.
Fog clings to the glass panes:
sticky cobwebs torn apart
            remain floating –
Where are the spiders?

Something swirls
            and swirls
pulling us closer
            to the Juan de Fuca Strait.
The foghorn blows
louder each time
making us think
of hoarse sheep
and frogs by marshy fields.
The foghorn sounds closer
each time, warning us
of Trial Island – we can't see
the blue-bottle-greenish light
flashing anymore, never mind
the four skinny poles lit up
with red lights.
We imagine everything
through the bud-taut branches –
our sunroom is adrift
            in the fog.

We've heard about those who never
returned from these waters
we've heard about those who
were rescued. We should be quiet.
Maybe the dead
have different rules
over here.
Maybe there are others
adrift in these currents.

Although She's a Small Woman

Although
she's a small woman
she can make
the fog leave Quatsino Sound.

Watch her now
without her clothes
she stands at the front
of the canoe – the waves
become lullabyes
as she sweeps her arms
to the north, to the south –
Her wrists are so alert
her song so sharp
the fog decides to lift
itself up and go
somewhere else.

And southward on the shore
there's the turtle-crow-man
the tall cedar man
waiting for this fog –
he likes to swallow
whole cloudy strips.

Ages later a Japanese girl
will poke that faded
turtle, fearing splinters
from the cedar, she'll be
surprised to feel skin
like soap, like fog,
as if a bolt of silk hardened
into wood
she can run her hands down.

'Man Swept out to Sea
as Huge Wave Hit Rock'

– Times-Colonist, Victoria, BC, 7 January 1992

Freak waves, rollers,
tsunami… tsunami…
Harbour waves.
Tidal waves out of the blue
they say it happens
from time to time.

Soon the wave felt heavy,
entangled with legs and arms
that were too slow –
and the fish felt a man
flailing against sea weed –

It's reported the rock he stood on
was 15 metres high,
that he was 56 years old,
and he stood 13 metres away
from the shoreline.
But can they make a graph,
a sketch, can they find
the proper equation? Can they tell us
what to do
so it won't happen again?

Was the sky too blue
that day in Ucluelet? How cold
was the water? Why did the wave pounce,
why take him away so he was never
found? Why must such a perfect
meditation be rent, rent body and soul
through and through
so you and I shiver, pull each other
nearer to the shore when we
walk by the same place.

When the Dead Feel Lonely

*When a Haida is drowned it is believed that his spirit
is translated to the body of a killer-whale. These whales
were therefore formerly much honoured, and never killed
by the Haidas. The appearance of one of them off the shore
in front of an Indian's dwelling is always regarded as a 'call'
to some member of the household, who will shortly meet
with his death by drowning.*

– Charles Hill-Tout

This is the time of year
when the dead feel lonely.

Who will go
        to keep them company?

Today the ocean
is a cold blackish grey –
but the waves flash bright.

The orcas swim blackly
in their black and white skins.

Who will go to keep them company?

The first person who meets their eyes?
The first person who hears their speech?

This is the time of year
when the women hide –
afraid to look
at an ocean swelling with orcas.

But I don't mind.
I've been watching them for days.
They are all I have now –

Look at the slow one
who keeps stopping, then stands upright
in the water and moves his head
as if he were searching for someone.

What can I do
        when my dead feel lonely?
Today I'll try to look deeper into their eyes.

9

How Far East is it Still East?

One Japanese fishing boat lost at sea
was found with a skeleton
curled up inside.

What happened to the others?

Nights when it was windy
the whales could hear the rattling bones.

How could so many Japanese
fishing boats get lost?

There were rules in 1639, rules
about the size of the boat,
rules about how much food
they could carry –

Food enough to make a man
turn back home,
            hungry.

How far east is it still east?
And how far west is it still west?

Somewhere in the North Pacific
the waters part

the waters part
only because we think they do –
but how could the ocean
really be split in two?

Where are your stars?
And where is your sky?

Which way do the waters part
for you? Which way will you let
the currents take you?

Now what is this voice that says:
'Go away. This is not
your world. You can't enter
this water – it's too dark for you.'

Only the whales listen
to the skulls trapped
in the Japanese fishing boats.

Now what is this voice that says:
'Go away. This is not your world.
Only the whales can answer
the lost fishermen.'

How far east is it still east?
And how far west is it still west?

Which way will you let the currents take you?

Of course, the women saw them first.
The women on their way
to collect wood –
the women on their way
to begin something –

At night they will whisper
to their elders:

Today two men walked out
of the sea – we watched them
eating berries – we do not know

if they are really human.
Today we saw fifteen whales
not far from the place
where the men walked out
           of the sea –

The Three Sisters

The tidal waves are believed by the Haidas to be caused by three sisters
who dwell on the West Coast. When they are annoyed in any way they revenge
themselves by raising these great waves and smashing the canoes of the Haidas
and drowning their occupants. The devil-doctor is the only intermediary between
the sisters and the people, and his services must be well paid for before he acts.

– Charles Hill-Tout

Rage is such a pure emotion.
We relish it. It's a way
to keep the Ocean clean.

I am the one –
I am the other –
And I am the last.

Yes, we are the three sisters –
and there is nothing unreal
about us. Being three we are

well-suited for strife, dialectical
dilemmas – Being three we can never
agree and in the end all we need

is to speak instead to the waves,
to find release in crashing walls
of water: a roar to match

the roiling anger in our throats.
I am the one who smells their fish.
I am the other who calls the wind.

I am the last who wakes the waves
who slakes my thirst
for the tug and pull of the tides.

Rage is a type of elation.
We relish it. It's the way we mean
to keep the Ocean clean.

Don't send us your devil-doctor.
He can't talk to us.
And what shall we do with him?

Don't send us your devil-doctor.
We can't love him.
He can't bring back the men

we loved when we were women,
mortal like you. The men we loved
drowned in the first freak waves

on a day before time
could be trapped and counted.
So don't send us your devil-doctor.

He won't know how to walk with us.
We are not human. We are not ghosts.
But we are real. We are surreal.

And we know how to keep the Ocean clean.
I am the one who smells their fish.
I am the other who calls the wind.

I am the last who wakes the waves
who slakes my thirst
for the tug and pull of the tides.

I am the last who watches
the one who eats their fish.
I am the last who hears

the other who sings with the wind.
I am the last who never hungers
who never sings –

I am the last who lives on pain,
who licks and licks the bitter taste
in my heart so I'll never forget

that day I couldn't stop weeping.
I am the last who needs to watch
how the Ocean swallows your men.

The Wild Woman of the Forest

spoke to Emily Carr
who loved her laughter –
full of fiddlehead-fern-light it was, this laughter,
full of spider webs and black water. It felt
like roe, salty under the tongue.

What could Emily do but follow?
The wild woman of the forest
showed her the way
from one totem pole to the next –
canoes slid through rain and fog
and Emily painted canvas after canvas
so unselfconsciously – cedar-bear-mother
eagle frog raven man cedar-man
bear-man eyebrows beaks claws
and beneath it all, the texture of wood.

Honest witness, attentive witness –
Emily left herself outside the picture
but her true self was always there –
too pure to be spotted.

Now it's too late.
You have to go to a museum
and imagine how the totem poles
once lived with the trees.

Polish-German Woodcarver Visits Vancouver Island

for Hannes and Jutta

Arbutus, ash, cedar
Douglas fir –
and most of all, driftwood.
He takes whatever strikes
his shoes, his fancy –
whatever lies unwanted on the ground.

A walk is not a walk
without his knife flinging slivers
of wood, left right and centre
along the way.

The blade peels, scours,
gouges uphill and down –
the blade wants
to hide away in wood.

His hands balance
the trees and the sky
differently from you and me.

Whether a piece of wood
will give a fish
or a man with a sharp face
is something only the knife knows.

Meanwhile the road
keeps winding. His young sons
dart back and forth.
Meanwhile his wife watches
starlings with beaks full
of parsley, build a nest.

Whether the wooden man
will carry a duck
in his arms, or a baby seal

with a strange tail
is something
only the knife knows.

Maybe the time of year matters.
For example,
it is April now.
Maybe the thin moon
meddles with more advice.

His hands
understand stories
hidden to us.
When he goes
to meet a totem pole
you can be sure
the knife burns.

Victor, Whiskey, Juliet, 2 2 3

When the steering gave out, the woman in the driver's seat
felt very calm, very numb. She didn't see
her entire life flash by her. She didn't curse the rented car.
As soon as she realized the steering didn't work anymore
she stopped listening to her full-of-instructions husband,
she stopped glancing at her little girl in the back seat.

She wished the eagle watching from the pine tree
would make a noise. But there was only the sound
of rain, first rain after a dry spell.
And then it felt as if the cells in her brain
had switched on Glenn Gould –
very slow and soft at first – then loud,
a rainstorm racing down the mountain.
She felt the piano, sharp: surgery
without anesthesia in her brain –
the notes like cold stones being dropped
while she held on to the useless steering wheel.
Downhill on a mountain road
one hairpin curve after another
connecting Tofino to Port Alberni. The car slammed
into the mountain, then bounced back against
the steel girder on the cliff edge, back and forth
four times, maybe five, while Glenn Gould played on
in her mind – each note matching the car's movement.
It didn't occur to the woman to be grateful
for the absence of oncoming traffic,
for the fact that it was Sunday morning,
meaning: no logging trucks.

When the car slid into a sandy spot and stayed
stuck beside the mountain, that was lucky
for there was no girder now by the cliff on the other side
of the road. And there was the Kennedy River
far down below curling towards the wall of the cliff.
The front wheels looked cross-eyed
the way they pointed towards each other.
A Native woman brought help
and the policemen looked surreal

17

because they smiled a lot, saying: 'You're alive,
you're alive! We didn't think you'd be alive.'

The birds were silent. The eagle could be seen flying.
And was Mr Death still lurking around behind the trees?
Another car had to be rented. The woman had to drive on
and she was still calm – or was it numb?
Only much later, six months later,
did the dreams start. Dreams of falling
while being locked in a car –
simply falling endlessly down, down –
And dreams of bungee jumping:
jumping off and realizing too late there's no rope.

Soundless, voiceless dreams.

Salt Spring Island

for Phyllis Webb

You wore purple
and Salt Spring Island flashed
green through your windows.

The way you spoke the words you spoke
reminded me of Gandhiji.

And then it was time
to catch the ferry back to Swartz Bay.

Even today I find Gandhiji's words green like yours
green like Salt Spring Island –
Those words live with your eyes
flashing and your purple blouse gentle
gentle in my mind, your colours
your words – and now I've put a paintbrush
in your left hand.

Your Sorrow

You take your sorrow with you when you leave.
However wide the sea or sky between,
the journey's end will bring you no reprieve.

– Peter Sacks

But what if you change
and your sorrow becomes
your memory, a broken bone,
a finger that heals strangely
forever crooked for the world to see
so even your thoughts don't match up –
and yet there's no pain left.

Isn't there a place
that would make you forget?
A sky that would make you
disagree with yourself – ?
A sea that would toss
your sorrow back in your face
shattered into a hundred,
a thousand different questions?

I don't know.
Is it reprieve
the journey's end should bring?
Or is it enough
simply to have gone away –
to have gone away so far
for so long that finally reprieve
is too gentle a word, too one-sided
for what you need,
for what you've already stepped toward.

I I
New World Dialogues

I am nothing. I am a man. I see. I know.
I began to see when I was not yet born;
when I was not in my mother's arms, but inside
my mother's belly. It was there that I began
to study about my people.

Sitting Bull (1834-1890)
from the *New York Herald Tribune* interview
with Sitting Bull, 16 November 1877.

The color used for the paintings had little to do
with what I had seen – the color grew as I painted.

Georgia O'Keeffe

What's yr race
  and she said
what's yr hurry
how 'bout it cock
        asian man
I'm just going for curry.

You ever been to ethni-city?
How 'bout multi-culti?

  You ever lay out skin
  for the white gaze?

Fred Wah

The Light Teased Me

for Georgia O'Keeffe

The light teased me
    all day –
the light made me
    doubt every word.
What do I mean? What
    have I gleaned
        so far?

By late afternoon
when I stumbled across
your *Red Poppy*
I couldn't see
    the *Poppy* anymore.

Instead, a fat tarantula emerged
rich with eggs, I could tell
by the way she moved.

A black sheen of joy.

Then she slid back into scarlet
    scraps of silk.

Cow's Skull – Red, White and Blue

There's something very right about it.

It's truthful, direct,
to the point – but also awkward,
ugly, brutal.

Imperfectly perfect.

Red blood.
White bones.
Blue sky.

When all the young men in America
could only think of Europe,

she walked through New Mexico
collecting bones.

Red blood.
White sky.
Blue bones.

Those days she gathered horses' skulls
and cows' skulls instead of flowers.

I see her staring at the skulls,
looking through the eye-holes –
            for hours.

Red sky, blue sky,
red blood
white bones, white sky –

She understood the land.
And when she left that place of dry heat
she took a barrel full of bones
back to New York.

Skinnydipping in History

for John Ashbery

First, you think of water and then, of course, the surface of the water.

Arms reaching out for air, for light, breaking the glassed-in-water-
picture of trees.

It's best to begin in the middle of the story: to plunge right in

to the heart of things, to the sort of place where dolphins can be found –
if you know what I mean.

There was the young man born in Japan but not Japanese
who spent his youth in Chile, who spoke of skinnydipping day after day
with his sixteen-year-old schoolmates, studying the light on naked limbs
while his mother planned dinner parties for Allende. Things happened
so quickly
as they always do. Afterwards, when they searched Allende's body
they found that boy's father's phone number. You bet they dialled that
number endlessly
to find out why. That boy, who's not such a young man anymore
once recalled Chile in a long sentence beginning with skinnydipping one
afternoon
and ending with Allende's death and the telephone no one wanted to
answer.

So much action in one sentence, so much noise.

One has to return to the surface for air.

There is so much we know, too much, cruelly, to be expressed in any medium,
Including silence. And to harbor it means having it eventually leach under

Your deepest thoughts will come to nothing if they don't surface.

There's something to be said for waiting for that most wanted

that most desired thing (whatever it is) to surface.

If you start thinking of the surface as *a visible core,*

not superficial but a visible core, it'll make you forget the knife.

After all, why would you need to cut through the core? What do you
think you'd find?

25

Don't we all know how even what you eat changes the surface of your
   skin.

It's true. You are what you eat: **Der Mensch ist, was er ißt**.

All of a sudden one realizes that *a yak is a prehistoric cabbage*.

If you have ever seen the glaring yaks in Ladakh eyeing the vegetables,

while the prehistoric smell of cabbage being cooked engulfs you as you
   walk by

the houses in Leh, then you'll understand the importance of the surface.

In fact, *the one thing that can save America*

is a slant version, a new mythology, a revision of its surface.

So what if *the juice is elsewhere*.

One day the juice might seep through and jazz up the surface.

One day a man will make a gesture you have never seen before.

One day a man will touch a piano in a way you never thought possible.

And how will the houses in Connecticut look then?

Will there still be people with big backyards

and green lawns to mow all summer?

Parrots

for Frida Kahlo

My parrots have been quiet all morning.
They've been eyeing yours, Frida.

Yes, life can be a watermelon
cut-open-juicy-red-bursting with black seeds.

But my parrots want mangoes:
hard green ones that are sour and white inside.

Your parrots look so happy, Frida, so well-fed.
They sit with their blue and yellow feathers puffed out.

My parrots long for yours, Frida, and they long for you;
for your eyes which make them believe in everything

and for your voice which makes them feel wanted and well-fed
even though, these days, there are no mangoes to be found.

What Does the Flower of Life Say, Frida Kahlo?

She says:
Five eggs have ripened
in my ovaries.
One is too big
and one is too little
and one is too sad
and one is too scared
but the last one
is very, very perfect.

She says:
Who's worried about the fizzy sperm?
Five eggs have ripened
in my ovaries –
but only one will manage
to stick itself inside
the wall of my womb –

The *Flower of Life* is red
and your three-eyed sun
is even redder, Frida,
and the earth too,
            all red –

And don't we all know
how red
a witch's egg can be.

Chutney

The diaspora women who thought Culture
meant being able to create
a perfect mango chutney in New Jersey
were scorned by the visiting scholar
from Bombay – who was also a woman
but unmarried and so different.
Sachi was her name, meaning 'Truth'.
And her greatest wish was to travel further north
to have a look
at Wallace Stevens' house. Once there

she circled the huge box-like wooden house
painted a dull white. It loomed.
It was far too awkward in the small yard.
She looked up
towards the trees, looked down at the road –
And her eyes
for once not analytical
became the eyes of the poorest Bombay woman
visiting a temple.

Nothing is Black, Really Nothing

1

nada es negro, realmente nada.
So Frida Kahlo wrote
one day in her diary.

But Frida, how black you could paint
your pulled-back hair, your braids,
and the little dark hairs above your lips –
How black your eyes
your eyebrows;
how black the hairs of your monkey
especially in *Fulang-Chang and I.*

But nothing is black.
True black that breathes
must shine with blue light,
green shadows – some say
a reddish glow means
the colour isn't black enough.

2

Then there was *elephantinum*,
elephant-tusk-black.
For Plinius records the tale
of Appelles, born
around 350 BC, he was
Alexander the Great's blue-blooded court painter –
he was the first
to create the colour called *elephantinum*
from fired ivory.

Dry distilled from tusks,
the fat fired out
from the elephant tusks…
and in the end black powder extracted,
distilled,
dry, dry…

And you can extract black
out of grape seeds.

And you can extract black
out of wood or gas
or out of that oil hidden deep within
the earth.

How black do you want
your paint?

3

I do not want
to consult the dictionary
for words about black.
I know those one-sided words
already: a black heart, a black mood,
a black day, a blunt black-jack –

I keep brooding instead
over my daughter's love for black –

How when she was not quite three
and the blond children teased her
for having brown hair,
she was only angered
by their inaccuracy.
'This is not brown!' she screamed
holding up a fistful of her hair.
'It's black!
My hair is black, black –
Not brown!'

As if to say
she knew her colours well.
She no longer confused orange with red,
indigo with violet,
or brown with black.
She could understand light green, dark green,
yellow, blue, she learned
        the names so quickly.

4

Now I keep turning back to you, Frida –
Nothing is black
but how you loved your black hair
that's not really black
and how many different black strokes
you found (when nothing is black)
to pull out every shade
        of blackness
from your hair, your self –

The Blue Snake Who Loves Water

for Michael

Outside
it's an Indian-summer-black
Iowa night.

Inside
I sleep alone
and I dream an afternoon picnic
in a tropical garden.

Outside
it's a harmless, flat
corn-fielded, dry night.

Inside
where I sleep alone
the grass is wet
and the blue snake
who loves water
has entered my dream.

'Watch out! A snake!'
everyone yells –
And it's strange
that I am not afraid.

The snake is on his way
to the lake. In no hurry
and yet, with no time to waste
he slides towards us –
everyone runs away
but I see no reason to move
or even to sit up
for he can easily slip
over me, which he does
sliding across my right shoulder
and pressing against my neck
as he leaves.

Outside
it's morning, already hot
this Iowa-bright prairie air.

Inside
I'm wide-awake – the tea steeps
and my neck burns
at the very spot the snake
touched as he slid
over me.

Outside
I meet my love
by the Iowa River.
We talk about dreams
about snakes – we have just met
a few weeks ago.

Still, I try to explain
the blueness of the snake
the burning on my neck –
How can a dream
be more than a dream?

No one will ever
believe me.

No one, except maybe the river.

Last week the river was a muddy slur.

But now full of blue sky
the river bends and smiles
and becomes a 'she'.
The river narrows
her metallic glinting eyes
sun struck – the river smiles
as if she could believe
in my blue snake.

The river smiles
as if she felt the blue snake
rushing through her.

Pelvis with Moon

A pelvis bone has always been useful
to any animal that has it –
quite as useful as a head, I suppose.

– Georgia O'Keeffe

The desert sky when it's blue sliding into grey
and when it's seen through a cow's pelvis bone –

That cow gave birth, gave milk
gave birth, gave birth – how many times?

The desert moon
was indifferent to the cow
as it is now indifferent to the bone.

And a woman drawn to this dry
indifference – full of desert heat and cold.

A woman walking for miles, for days,
grateful for the strength
of her own pelvis bone.

Does she think of birth?
       Of death? What does she want?

She who feels the meaning of the sky,
of the moon behind the pelvis bone –

What does she think?

She who watches the meaning of the pelvis bone
when it is held and held
like that so the holes are focused:
       sucking in the sky.

It Has Come to This

The Chiefs:
Rain in the Face
Red Cloud
Long Dog
Charging Hawk
Young Man Afraid of His Horses
Crow Foot
Kicking Bear

In a museum, in a German city
I greet your photographs.
Your names give me a story
I can't write,
a story I can only dream
on warm nights.

Burial of the Dead
at the Battle of Wounded Knee S.D.
CopyRighted Jan. 1st 1891
by the North Western Photo Comp.
Chadron Neb. No.1.

Who owns the dead? Who owns
the burial? What would you say
Sun in the Pupil
Red Shirt Girl
Has a Dog
Spotted Thunder
Cast Away and Run
Wounded in Winter
Shedding Bear
Shake the Bird
Bring Earth to Her?

Your names are stuck
in my mind – I want to keep
them: I want to imagine the eyes, teeth,
voices, fingers – that lived in your names.

III
The Stinking Rose

The proper response to a poem is another poem.
                                    Phyllis Webb

So art does not labour.
I took my time. Here. Now you take it.
                                    Patrick Lane

The Stinking Rose

Everything I want to say is
in that name
for these cloves of garlic – they shine
like pearls still warm from a woman's neck.

My fingernail nudges and nicks
the smell open, a round smell
            that spirals up. Are you hungry?
Does it burn through your ears?

Did you know some cloves were planted
near the coral-coloured roses
to provoke the petals
into giving stronger perfume...

Everything is in that name
            for garlic:
Roses and smells
            and the art of naming...

What's in a name? that which we call a rose,
By any other name would smell as sweet...

But that which we call garlic
smells sweeter, more
vulnerable, even delicate
if we call it *The Stinking Rose.*

The roses on the table, the garlic in the salad
and the salt teases our ritual
tasting to last longer.
You who dined with us tonight,
this garlic will sing to your heart
to your slippery muscles – will keep
your nipples and your legs from sleeping.

Fragrant blood full of garlic –
yes, they noted it reeked under the microscope.

His fingers tired after peeling and crushing
the stinking rose, the sticky cloves –
Still, in the middle of the night his fingernail
nudges and nicks her very own smell
            her prism open –

Ninniku

1

Ninniku, ninniku
the Japanese said
as they examined the Buddhist
monks. *To bear insults
with patience* on the way to Nirvana.

The Buddhist mind
is strengthened by the sharp
light of garlic.

White... White... is the flame of garlic
        the heat of garlic.

Then Queen Maya, Siddhartha's mother
dreamt that a white elephant
entered her womb.

White –

And that was the colour of the swan
Siddhartha rushed to save.

White –

And that was the colour
of Kanthak, the horse he once rode.

White –

And that was the colour
of the elephant he once rode.

The Japanese met Buddhism
and *ninniku* sprouted
along with the lotus.

om mani padme hum
the monks whispered
ever sleepless, ever vigilant,
every day they walked for miles –

for the body must be able
to bear the Truth,
for without the body the mind can not
climb the steep path of right mindfulness.

om mani padme hum
the monks whispered
with garlic on their breath.

2

Ninniku:
To bear insults with patience.
That's what they have to do,
those immigrants
from the garlic-eating regions.
Some travel north
and some travel west
but they all learn to keep their distance.

Sometimes the women
     in desperation
douse themselves with perfume –
musky jasmine
     husky rose –
later on the bus, humid
vapours mingle with garlic
on their skin and clothes; only sharpen
the luminous
homesickness
in the whites of their eyes.

रसोन (*Russown*)

लहसुन की जड़ में चरपरा रस
(*lahsoon ki jad mai charpara russ*)
पत्तों में कड़वा रस
(*patto mai kadva russ*)
नाल में कषैला रस,
(*nal mai kashaila russ*)
नाल के अग्रभाग में क्षार रस
nal kay agrabhag mai kshar russ)
तथा बीजों में मधुर रस रहता है।
(*tatha bijo mai madhur russ rahta hai*)

— Ayurvedic text

In the roots of garlic
there is hot, spicy juice,

चरपरा रस (charpara russ) **तीखो २स** (tikkho russ)

Fire: hot breath from the dry earth –
soil where the cobra lives
soil where the roots sting.

In the leaves of garlic
there is bitter juice,

 કડવો ૨સ (kadvo russ).

Bitter leaves,
bitter from the hard earth.
Shards of clay, bones of cattle –
bitter green numbs
the hungry widow.

In the stem of garlic
there is astringent,
ambla tasting, turmeric tasting juice:
कषैला रस, तूरो रस
(kashaila russ, turo russ)

43

The stem tries to run away from the roots.
The stem becomes seductive
the stem has a taste
that will make you an addict.

In the uppermost parts of the stem
            of garlic
there is a salty juice,
લવણ રસ, ક્ષાર રસ
(lavann russ, kshar russ)

Beloved salt –
salt for the sparkle in your eyes
and salt for the blood.
The uppermost parts of the stem of garlic
will keep you enslaved
with your beloved salt.

And in the seeds of garlic
there is sweet juice:

મધુર રસ (madhur russ).

Born with such sweet hope –
sweet seeds, one could never have imagined
milk and honey-sweet seeds of garlic.

On this earth there are six juices

called રસ (russ).

Garlic has all of them except
for the sour juice,

अम्ल रस (amal russ).

That is why those who understood garlic

named it रसोन (russown).

On this earth garlic has five
juices – once again
the number five.

Garlic in War and Peace

In peace they rubbed garlic paste
across their lower backs
before they lay together.
A slow cleansing – it was
sticky, then strangely cool.
It was their secret bite
their strongest aphrodisiac.
And they preferred green garlic
with large purple cloves.

In war they dabbed garlic paste
over each wound –
such endless wincing
and endless those white cotton bandages.
The stench of pus and garlic
finally giving way to pink skin
shiny as a freshly peeled clove
of garlic – new patches of skin
reminding them how in peace
their garden overflowed with lilies
and garlic – and the roses!
The roses sprayed with garlic-water.

In peace their only war
was against the worms.

Mars Owns this Herb

And so the Romans said:
    May you not eat garlic
meaning: *May you not be drafted*
    into the army –

Human ways haven't changed much.

In 1916 the British government asked for garlic
and they paid a shilling for each pound of it.

And the trenches were always full
of wounded limbs, broken limbs covered
with sterilized sphagnum moss
    soaked in garlic juice.

And maybe there was one man – I imagine him
barely twenty – who thought of the Romans
as he watched the skin on his legs
become less grey and begin to heal.

A Touch of Coriander

Garlic is believed to act as an aphrodisiac
when pounded with fresh coriander
and taken with neat wine.

– Gaius Pliny the Elder

It is the coriander – the green leaves
that cool the tongue
after garlic. It is the coriander: feathery, tender,
that makes them undress each other
before they've finished undressing the garlic –

And the wine? With garlic
the wine only makes them thirstier –
the wine only makes the kiss last longer.

And then they'll turn
again to coriander – the green leaves
that soothe the eye-lids.

47

Bear's Garlic at Nevern

for G.C.

'Look, look!' You call out
        as you run:

your fingers stained dark red
        shiny with blood
        from the yew tree –

Then, after a quick glance
to make sure
no one is watching, you pull out
some green leaves.

        Yes, you're the strong one,
          you're the fast one –

And your clean
movement brings up
        white roots
soft and suddenly free
of mud.

We gather bear's garlic, wild Wood Garlic,
ramsons, almost like Lily of the Valley –
hard umbels all green
spread out clusters of springy stars –

We sniff our hands:
a smell of yew-tree sap, blood thick
        and wild garlic.

Oh but we're not done yet –
we have to walk through
the overgrown paths – tall grass slaps
        wet against our legs.
Wild flowers sprout at crooked
odd angles, they slant over,
trying to shelter the gravestones –
from what?

I want to take a bite from the garlic,
even a tiny bite will do –
but I don't.

Should I taste
what grows in a graveyard?

You find strawberries.
We eat them.
This is how the sun tastes
when it's allowed to enter fruit.
This time I don't hesitate.

A swirl of strawberries curl
           in and out
almost hidden by leaves and stones.
We eat them – balancing the garlic stems
           in our hands –
balancing all we promise to plant,
we circle the church. The flooded river
is loud. It gushes in such a hurry.
Rapid, gurgling muddy noise
drags along broken things.

We circle the Great Cross.
We must touch it.
A sort of lingam slab – thirteen feet high.
Cross after cross entwined:
a patterned undergrowth –
a defiant, endless weave.

And then you point into the shadows
at a stone-carved face
I would have missed.

Such a small face. Too small.
I wish it larger.
I want the whole body –
so you imagine her,
give me her mood
illuminating your secret:
It's too simple to say
she's having sex, you decide,
if that is Sheila na Gig

she's enjoying herself in labour.
She's lost in herself, lost
in the soon-to-be-born.
How else
could she give birth?

I turn to you,
tasting strawberries on my tongue –

and still this craving for wild garlic
I try to ignore
so I step closer to the desire-filled face –
the stone-life,
rain-worn but wild
on that skin of Sheila na Gig.

What else can I call her
so you know how I feel?

Isn't she the one
we came to meet?
Our *Devi* of strawberries and garlic –

Frightened Bees

Notes from a Welsh Herbal

Take a clove of garlic
prick in three or four places in the middle
dip in honey and insert in the ear
covering it with some black wool.

And if I had no black wool
would white wool do –
or must it be at least red
or dark blue?

Let the patient sleep
on the other side every night
leaving the clove in the ear
for seven or eight nights unchanged.
It will prevent the running of the nose
and restore the hearing.

Black wool I found at last
but it makes me dream
of frightened bees with a dead queen –
        homeless
swarms rushing in a panic –

night after night – the dead queens
are piling up fast – but someone wants
to crush them with rose petals
and honey – someone wants to eat
the dead queens and taste
a sweetness,
        a knowledge no one dares to try.

Ther is No Rose of Swych Virtu

Ther is no rose of swych virtu
as is the rose that bar Jhesu

   – Anonymous, England, fifteenth century

An old gardener plants a rosary
of garlic around the rosebushes.

And the sun on the high windows
makes the song softer,
softer – a hum in his ears:

ther is no rose of swych virtu...

while the odours from the dug up earth
cling to the air – and the wind
leaves no boundaries between the scent
of roses and the scent of garlic.

The Worm

I know about you.
You hate me. You think too much.
And you like to imagine me
       biting into a clove of garlic.

What do you expect?

It burns – it burns.

I know *Allicin:* reactive pungent
unstable
strongly medicinal. I know you.
You think the garden belongs to your kind.
Today you've spread white fire
over my home – garlic all
over me – I try to rub it off
in the grass – but do you know the red rose
is still my love –
my love, not yours.

A Poem in Three Voices

Today I've become an angel.
I've no need for garlic now.
I wish I could tell my mother
to stop crying
I wish I could thank her
for the coin she put in my hand,
folding my dead fingers
over it – she made sure
I would be ferried across
the River Styx.
I wish I could thank my mother
for the garlic she put
in my dead mouth
before they buried me –
Yes, it was the garlic
that helped me grow angel wings.

Over here they keep asking me
to tell them what happened.
But even I don't know.
I had climbed up the apple tree
and then I saw *him* swooping down:
The oldest man – but Sibyl-faced, scrawny
and dressed in the blackest black.
His huge leathery wings were oily,
filthy with blood – and even his lips
were black. That was the last thing I saw:
his lips, his black snarl.

2 *Second voice:*

What have I done
to deserve this fate?
They found my boy crumpled
in the orchard – his throat
mangled, his face bloodless –
Why has the earth betrayed me?
Why is my crop of garlic useless?

3 *Third voice:*

The boy stank of garlic.
I didn't touch him.
There he sat like a monkey in a tree
all elbows and knees and he had
beautiful teeth.
But it was clear he lived with garlic.
It had already entered his blood
while he kicked about in his mother's womb.
And she, wise woman, kept cloves
of garlic beneath her pillow.
That boy had been breast-fed
with garlicky milk –
and as he grew older he ate garlic
with every meal.

No way would I touch him.
He simply fell.
When he saw me he lost his balance.
He fell and broke his neck.
I left – but someone must have seen me.
For no one believes me
and now the whole village
is after me.

A Brahmin Wants the Cows
to Eat Lots of Garlic

So he can drink
the garlic-rich milk.

That's the only way
he's allowed to take garlic.

For three days and three nights
he'll wait, let the garlic seep into
the cows, he'll wait for the right moment.

A brahmin wants the cows
to eat lots of garlic –
so he watches and he sings *bhajans*
making sure they do.

He wants to step out
of his brahminhood and wander
cow-like through the spring-hazy-purple dust,
        cow-dust.

But a little bit of milk
will bring him back to his senses.

If You Named Your Daughter Garlic
Instead of Lily or Rose

She would travel far
to gather mushrooms –

After a night of rain
she would rescue snails,
putting them back on the broad leaves,
the high stems able to support them.

She would never lose
a crop of tomatoes.

You would never know
she was Garlic
because she would smell of roses –
her garden overflowing with fennel –
She would travel far
to gather mushrooms, that daughter
you named Garlic.

And unlike Tolstoy's Varenka
she'll meet a man
who won't mind
talking about mushrooms.

Self-Portrait with Garlic

In the kitchen – cloves of freshly peeled garlic.
Sound of a knife being sharpened.
April late afternoon light –
      light filtered through green trees.

How shall I do it?

Watercolour? Oil? Charcoal?

Colour or black & white?

Or, a self-portrait in words.
How shall I do it?

The look on my face
      is not a mask –
am I absorbed in the garlic or lost
in the book I stopped reading
before entering the kitchen?

And there's a radio on the table.
Has it been turned on? There's the sound
      of my four-year-old daughter
running in and out of the kitchen.

Oh but the garlic is everywhere –
large spring bulbs in the basket:
their stalks, thick green
their cloves covered with purplish skin.
And chopped up cloves on the cutting-board –

Now my face has changed –
my eyes are different because
      of the garlic.

It is a difference one can't even photograph.

Allium Moly *and Odysseus*

First, there was *Moly*:
Black was the stem,
milky-white the flowers
of this strong smelling, divine herb
that Hermes found in the grass
for Odysseus.

Only the gods had access to *Moly*.

But there is no *Moly* in Nature.

Should you care to look
you'll find *allium moly*:
a daylight-green stem
with sparks of yellow flowers –

Imagine Odysseus with *allium moly*:

There he stood
in the doorway
clutching this yellow-flowered herb
hidden within his garments.

His thumbnail digging in
almost crushing the last of his yellow
garlic – and Circe
had a bad cold,
she couldn't smell a thing –
not even the pigs around her.

There he stood:
impatient Odysseus
counting his days on the island,
wondering how long
his garlic-fed luck
would last – how long
a little bit of *allium moly*
can fight magic
with more magic.
How long before Circe
recovers the power
of her nose – and finally realizes
why her spells have failed –

Instructions to the Artist

How can I know
    what I want?

Paint me some garlic.
The whole plant
    shaken by footsteps
the whole plant full of movement
with your paint.

Maybe I need more
than garlic – paint me a full red rose
somewhere in a corner
across from the garlic.

Of course you'll know
how to arrange the space:
the movement of the garlic
    the swaying rose –
then stillness somewhere
and tension and balance –
I'll leave that up to you.

But how about the human figure?
Can you include it somehow
    with the garlic and the rose?

I don't mean just any human figure –

A First Draft from the Artist

You've painted a thin man
with his hands raised high
so high – is he walking
slowly or is he just
standing – nowhere to go?

Oh he's a weird ghost
but he's not a ghost.
He's androgynous but he's not.
He's a secret hermaphrodite.
He's sexless but erotic in all
the non-erogenous zones.

This man is brown,
tanned from the sun
yellow glares behind him –

and his heart
can be seen through his chest:
bright red – fresh blood
a heart-shaped lump
like a head of garlic
balanced on its tip.

This man looks strong
for all his leanness.

And he holds up
a huge red rose in his right hand
and an enormous head of garlic
in his left hand.

Is the rose for Mary?
For every woman named Mary?
Can garlic only be held
in the left hand?

What does he mean by this?
Garlic streaked creamy yellow
and purple in his left hand –
and a happy red rose
fluttering in his right hand –

Why are his hands raised
so high?

Why have you painted a man
and not a woman?

The Man in the Artist's First Draft Speaks

I'm the sort of man who prefers
to work in the kitchen.
Not simply cooking –

I like to sit and read
in the kitchen.
I write letters – long letters
while sitting in the kitchen.

I've just started writing a novel
about a man who lives
in a kitchen.

What am I doing here
with this ripe rose and ready
to burst garlic?

Don't you dare think of me
        as a symbol.

The artist made me this way –
with my arms raised so high
as if I were waving to my love
on the other side of the garden.

The Good Farmer

The good farmer follows
the gypsy's advice and feeds garlic
to his sheep and horses, and puts sprigs
of wild garlic in the stables –

The good farmer knows
how to keep his horses
        from getting bewitched.

But should a gypsy smile
at the farmer's children, or linger
to stroke their heads
then he'll cross himself to break the spell
and he'll mutter: *Knoblauch, Knoblauch, Knoblauch,*

Knoblauch, Knoblauch, Knoblauch –

sometimes uncertain about the number
of times he should say *Knoblauch*.

A Wintry July in Bremen

It has been a cold July
with rain every day.

Today you show me
an enormous painting of garlic:
a full head partly open
with yellow from a winter sky

and lead pencil grey
       blue shadows.

I call it my giant-winter-garlic.
I look at it with eyes
that are tired of rain.

If you painted the cloves
of garlic even larger than this
I would see those cloves
       turn into canoes
propped up
slanting against pine trees
on a night when the moon is
swollen with light, the full curve
of a milk-heavy breast
the full curve
of a child-heavy belly –

On a night
like this the fishermen move restless –

A few have gone out
to their canoes – they are so silent
even as they touch the water.

Rosehips in August

The half-open, half-empty head of garlic
curls out in every direction
like an old rose, still large and strong –
not at all worm-eaten –
but just heavy with its own
half-fermented smell.

Rosehips and garlic are strewn across
the table in your painting:
A pale flush of scarlet
translucent watercolour
        beside a dark garlic leaf.

I am drained of thoughts
        of words, of speech –
I only want to fill myself
        with colours.

Your pen, fine as a needle –
the sharp nib,
the sharp smell in your rooms…

Afternoons we drink rosehip tea,
hot red and pungent
        against this cold spell.

Through your window
I can see rosehips ripening,
ripening – and in the rainy wind
they fling themselves against the glass.

If a Ghazal were like Garlic

It would be a place
where the *Duende* lived.

If you sang this ghazal
it would heal your vocal cords.

No matter how much you pulled
and tore out your voice

and spread your arms, tense-tendoned
your hands fisted, fingers cold-knuckled –

No matter how deep the song cut
into your eyes, your bones,

no matter how much the song
tightened around your neck

the ghazal's sounds would heal
your wounds.

Garlic and Sapphires in the Mud

Dark blue stones.
White cloves of garlic.
The earth begins to soften again.

Dark blue flowers,
the colour of sapphires,
grow beside the garlic.
The mud is deep –

His shoes sink in deeper
and deeper with each step
as he tries to pull out
the bedded axle-tree.

His hands flush red.
With mud-stained palms
he stands between broken garlic stalks,
stones and flowers –

Flowers torn by the axletree.

There is birdsong,
birdcries that his blood follows.

It's only when he turns
around so you can see his face
that you realize he's old.
Heroically old – with a broken
face – the scars dividing up
forehead and mouth
more than they should.

It's only when he turns
around so you can see his face
that you wonder *where* he's been.

But the earth has begun
to soften again –
And there is birdsong,
birdcries that his blood follows.

The Pharaoh Speaks

I feel heavy, sticky. I've been
too tightly bound and squeezed shut.

Still, how good it is to be alone
at last in my tomb –
Amidst all the gold and lapis lazuli
they've hidden six bulbs of garlic.

My soul has come back
for one last visit. My soul hovers
by the garlic and prays.

The gold laughs
and sings of its golden self –
daring my skin to achieve
            such a perfect colour.
The lapis lazuli tries to put a blue
            spell over me.

But the six bulbs of garlic remain self-contained –
quietly odourless,
saving their power for something else.

It Has Not Rained for Months

To know whether a woman will bear a child.
Clean a clove of garlic, cut off the top, place it
in the vagina and see if next day her mouth smells
of it. If she smells, she will conceive; if not, she will not.

– Hippocrates

It has not rained for months.
Hot dirt from the fields, hot dust
whipped up with the wind
hurts my throat, my chest –

I can not breathe
and then he comes with his clove
of garlic, with his hot garlicky breath
and his beard, sharper than thorns
and his face of stone – I can not breathe
but he opens my mouth

and then I must keep this clove
of garlic inside where my flesh
has become so raw
that it burns – It has not rained
for months – and I lie facing the window
and I watch the crows
peck at stolen seeds –
I can not breathe
and every morning he comes
full of remorse with his hot
garlicky breath he opens my mouth

and then I must remove
this clove of garlic
from this burning flesh
        and I think that if
I would bleed at least
the blood would heal
me, at least the blood
would soothe
        the garlic scrubbed cuts.

71

It has not rained for months.
I am wet from my own sweat.
Hot dirt from the fields
stuck in my heart.

Every month I bleed
too much –

too much – and then he comes
with his clove of garlic
and then I must keep
this clove of garlic deep inside me
where it burns.

IV
Old World Blood

What do you want appetites for: what do you want
anything for: there is no question of wanting, only
of giving expression to this cry, at that point where
you are living it as you give it expression, speech,
don't learn speech, speech can't be learnt, you can't learn
to speak clearly, the only honourable thing is utter failure.
Samuel Beckett

... Time's
power, the only just power – would you
give it away?

Adrienne Rich

An India of the Soul

It is not necessary to have poems full of mendicants and minarets, gurus and ghats, to contemplate an India of the soul.

– Alastair Niven

But the soul will be the colour of turmeric
        spilt on white stone.

And the creature who lives in the soul
will count with her thumb
on the joints of her fingers.

Time will be slow
and Time will be concrete
and Time will be stuck
like a wet crow peering down
from a tree, broken and black –

Who is more jagged, the tree or the crow?
The crow peering down, his head so crooked
        so tilted –

Then the soul will be the colour of ferns
        surrounded by mosquitoes.

And the creature who lives in the soul
will wash her feet
before going to bed.

A Gujarati Patient Speaks

A heart surgeon in London made it a practice
to operate only after he and his patient
had both listened to Gould recordings.

Usually, when I'm sick
I eat rice with yoghurt,
two cloves of raw garlic
and some દાળનું પાણી (dalnu pani).

After the dal has settled
on the bottom of the pot
I scoop out the top-water,
rich in onions and garlic –
I squeeze fresh lemon juice
over it in my bowl,
drink it slowly –
Usually, I feel much better.

Coriander is important.
And fenugreek.
I use lots of fenugreek.

Although I live in London
I still prefer my ways.
Sitar, tabla: I call them my basic
instruments because they help me
improve my mood, soothe my headaches.

When I hear certain notes
I can smell patchouli,
I can smell my mother's soap
and the oil she used
          on her hair.

So when my doctor asked me
to listen to all this Bach,
the *Goldberg Variations* –
I thought he must know
something about Ayurvedic methods.

But why Bach?
And why Glenn Gould?
Normally, I don't listen
        to piano.
Even my children prefer saxophone –
        and mostly jazz.

Still, this morning after breakfast
I gave it a try.
Glenn Gould: such movement, exact
the way honeybees measure
        and remeasure the sun
all summer – pink zinnias –
urgent wings hum after
the shifting angle of earth and sun.

And if there is sleep in the background
it is the sleep of a man
with too many dreams –
and it is the sleep of lovers
who can't ignore each other.

I can see why a surgeon
would worship the gestures.
lust after the fingers behind this sound.

But me? How will the piano
understand my moods?

शांति *(Shantih)*

Why did you latch on
      to that word
when you probably never used it
in common speech or prayer?

But maybe that's why.

To you
it sounded new
and holy – so holy.

While we who use it
use it for everything –
When we scold our children
      begging for quiet:

અરે શાંતિ રાખો !
(aray shantih rakho!)

હવે શાંતિથી બેસો !
(havay shantihthi beso!)

And our daily prayer
begins

      ॐ सह नाववतु ।
      (om saha naa vavatu)

      सह नौ भुनक्तु ।
      (saha nau bhunaktu)

then falls into

      ॐ शांतिः शांतिः शांतिः ।।
      (om shantih shantih shantih)

Everyday-words I took
for granted.

सह वीर्यं करवावहै ।
(saha veeryam karvaa vahai)

तेजस्वि नावधीतम् अस्तु ।
(tejasvinaa vadhitam-astu)

मा विद्विषावहै ।
(maa vidvishavahai)

The Sanskrit becomes so simple
when I translate it:

May the Lord protect both of us.
May He use both of us.
Let us both work together.
May our knowledge shine forth.
Let us not hate each other.
Let there be peace, peace, peace.

Does it sound deeper
if you call it *shantih*?
What is the true sound
of *shantih*?

The end of a war – any war?
Sometimes it's only a night
without bombs –

and sometimes, somewhere in a house
a house that's a burnt smallness –
broken glass
and no animals –
somewhere in a house
the sound of children sleeping
a sound that is so different
if one of them has only
one leg.

Genealogy

My daughter
when she was four
once described herself as a tiny egg,
so small, she was inside me
at a time when I was still not born
when I was still within her grandmother.
And so, she concluded triumphantly,
I was also inside Aaji.

When she showed me
her newest painting, she said:

At night the sun is black
and the moon turns yellow.
Look, that's how I painted it.
This is the sky at night
so the sun is also black.
What are the angels doing at night?
It's not bad to die
because then you can become
an angel – and you can fly and that's so nice –
I'll be happy to be an angel.

Later, I overheard her say to her father:

When I am a grandmother
I'll be very old
and you'll be dead.
But I hope you've learned
to fly by that time

because then you can
fly over to my house
and watch me with my grandchildren.

Black Swans for Swantje

Their wings are clipped.
That's why they stay
      over here.

Snow melts
and the first green
stems are crawling out
from the ground.
That's why they've started
to build a nest.

Red beaks snapping up
the straw left for them.
See how their necks move
like black snakes
dancing upright –
faster and faster,
back and forth…

What else is there to do?

The air smells of horses,
fertilized fields –

You will collapse
      hypnotized
if you stare at the swans
for too long.

As I say this
a flock of wild geese
flies overhead – they are loud
long arrows – taut
now a tight arc.

The swans wait, look up
tense with abruptly stopped
motion. As if the geese
were calling out to the swans:

as if the swans wished
they could follow the geese
and seek out some other lake
some other spot
which would at least be
of their own choosing.

One of the Wurst-Eaters on the Day After Good Friday

Bad Tölz, Bavaria, 30 March 1991.

Blutwurst in the morning
then off to the church on the hill
where he will pray kneeling
on the cold steps, flanked
with wooden banisters,
unvarnished and so dry –
upon which angels stand –
painted, winged children holding up candles,
Heilige Stiege leading to the altar.
An altar well-stocked with a holy skeleton
and bits of hair, bits of clothes
from a few good saints.

He will pray kneeling –
crawling up the twenty-eight steps
with a square pillow
for his knees and a different prayer
for each step.

Blutwurst in the morning
while it snows across the Alps
whitening all the farms
to the colour of *Speckfett*
and chilling the Tegernsee,
forcing all the fish
to swim deeper.

The puppies were born yesterday
but the pregnant mare waits
quiet. In a week or so
the farmer thinks while he cuts
Blutwurst in the morning.

Fate

i.m. A.K. Ramanujan (1929-1993)

Of course, you would smile
if you knew that I've decided
to insert fate
telepathy and unconscious 'second sight'
at the core of this poem.

Let fate be an elephant who needs water,
walking along the x-axis
and let telepathy be a young scorpion:
fast, hungry, scurrying down
the y-axis – we do not know,
perhaps we'll never know if they meet.
Only the monkey called *second sight* knows
and he won't tell us unless
we pass a certain test, unravel
a certain trick.

But how shall I explain
that day I dropped everything
that needed to be done,
turned instead to your books
started re-reading them
one after the other in a great rush
stayed up most of the night
alert, nostalgic,
I hunted out my favourite lines
not knowing that all the time
you lay in hospital.
Not knowing why
I had this sudden craving
for your words.

You were still in Chicago,
I in Bremen, and the Ganga still flows
dirty and oblivious.

Forgive me if I call it fate
or some form of telepathy.
But very soon the phone rang
at an odd hour with the news
of your death –
while your books were still strewn
around me so full of book-marks,

they bulged
some like paper flowers
some like paper birds
trying to open petals, wings –
little fans of magic
          with their own dreams
refusing to fit back
into the tight slots on the shelf.

Orpheus Confesses to Eurydice

1

It was a lack of faith.
I admit it. I didn't believe enough
in you or even in the power
of my song. I needed constant reassurance.
Yes, I saw how the Furies wept
as I sang slower, softer – Time stopped for me –
still, I didn't think they'd let you go.
I didn't think you'd be free to follow me.
And so I looked back
·wondering: *were you really there?*

I've caught the snake
that killed you – I keep him
alive. He's become a sort of pet –
such a small viper, and so supple –
my last connection to you. And his brightness:
eyes, skin – how he shimmers in the sun – keeps me alert
and reminds me at times of your brightness:
the sun in your hair, the jewels around your neck.

At first, of course, I thought of revenge.
I thought of hurting the snake,
          of throwing him into a fire.
But I hesitated and now I've grown fond of him.

2

Once when I stood singing by the cliffs
a sharp stone fell – and then a lizard
darted to the east and her sliced-off tail
rushed away to the west – and I watched
the tail shudder and jerk –
a yellow-green thing in such a hurry.

Now I've become a torn-off
lizard's tail. Only my tongue lives
in my bodiless head – my tongue still sings
against the noise of the river.

86

Maybe this is what I really wanted:
To be just a tongue –
a lizard's tail without the lizard.

To be a pure voice
without my tired, awkward body –

Now I'm almost weightless and about to be swallowed
by the ocean – I will become
                    a stronger voice.

Jealousy

I go to bed and then that man
sits in the next room and continues
laughing about his own writing.
And then I knock on the door
and I say, 'now Jim,
stop writing or stop laughing!'

— Nora Joyce

A woman eats her heart out
and the window near her bed is too small
and it won't shut
properly – and her heart tastes
quite sweet, very nice despite the bitterness –
but the moon doesn't care
and anyways the moon stopped
helping her long ago.

The opera is just over
and a crowd of footsteps,
so many high heels, clatter
past her window.

There are no stars tonight.
Only clouds that move
too quickly and make her dizzy.

She'll close her eyes
but she won't sleep
she'll continue to eat her heart
                out all night –

And in the morning she'll think of a way
to fix the window.

Kaspar Hauser Dreams of Horses

based on Werner Herzog's film

Roß, Roß, he growls his word for horse
scraping a wooden horse
             across the floor.

That's his only word
and he looks as if he's at least
forty. His feet are chained
he's half naked – covered with mud
and straw –
no one has taught him to walk.
Roß, Roß, is all he says
to his only toy.

One night, the old man: his keeper,
his father – lets him outdoors,
takes him into town
and leaves him there.

Someone takes him in –
helps him learn what he needs to know.

His dull eyes
his numb face
propped up with a white collar.
Black-suited and stiff
they take him out into the sun.

Here is a rose, they say
here is a tree.
Now look at this book.

And listen, listen,
they tell his numb face:
that is a bird.
This is a violin.

At last, one day
Kaspar Hauser has tears on his face.
This must be what they call shame, he thinks,
this salty wetness against
my skin – against my vision –
What are these tears for?

Life begins again for Kaspar Hauser
            and we begin to hope.

Finally we see his dreams
flickering on the screen:
out of focus dreams
coloured ochre and brown
filtered through an almost golden light.

Dreams of horses
            thousands of horses
or rather, soldiers on horseback –
soldiers riding into battle
kicking up yellow dust.

Where did he get such dreams?
Dreams he couldn't even understand –
thinking it all real at first.

What part of his soul
sheltered such horses?
And did he remember *Roß, Roß?*

Kaspar Hauser, who had to learn
the human meaning of tears –
how did he know about war?

Paula Modersohn-Becker Speaks to Herself

I will become amber.

Daphne wanted
to become a tree.
I think
it was she who chose sweet laurel,
she who chose leaves that are always green.

But I need to go
deeper, into amber.

Already this light,
this sunny May morning
        in Paris
has turned my hair amber
        the dark russet kind –
more red than gold.

My eyes: brownish amber
sparkle brighter than the necklace
I wear today – large oval
beads of amber – so heavy.

It's too warm, too early,
but never mind. I'm half-naked. It's easier
to paint what I mean to paint
        this naked way.

How would I look
if I were pregnant?
Like this? My nipples, still so pale
would also turn to amber.

And my blood?
I imagine it too will become stronger.
It will stop its rush-rush river sounds
it will stop pounding
my blood will become quiet
        silent –
and in the end
it will harden into amber.

My belly is so white!
So white!
How round should I make it?
How big will I get
when I'm with child?

Oh I will paint it round enough
so there will be no doubt
about my condition.

This is a self-portrait
of a pregnant woman
who secretly knows
she will become amber.

This is a self-portrait
in which I don't care
what anyone says.

Exactly five years ago today
we got married – Otto and I.
But this May I am alone
at last with my *self*.
My *self* that now only speaks
to me in Paris.

I need to live
            more fully through
the body to find my soul.

Yes, the body, this woman's body
                  that is mine –
I need to go deeper
into amber.

Should I have a baby?
And if I did?
Then, would my body be able
to teach my soul something new?

Ophelia in Defence of the Queen

after Marina Tsvetayeva

Prince Hamlet! I've had enough
of your stirring up the worm-ridden bed...
Can't you see the roses? Look!
Think of her
who's been counting her last days
just waiting for this particular day.

Prince Hamlet! I've had enough
of your degrading the Queen's womb,
that sweet aching, the way blood rushes
deep within the arc of bone and muscle
just to awaken skin – Have you ever
noticed all the different sorts of skin
that cover your body?
It's not for virgins to judge
such passion. Phaedra's guilt weighed heavier:
Even now
they can't stop singing of her.

And let them sing! But you, you're chalky,
mouldy. Save your curses for dead bones.
Prince Hamlet! Who do you think you are
to pass judgement on blood that burns?

But if... Well then, watch out! Up through the gravestones
and on – straight to the bedroom – to fall in bliss!
It is I who come to defend my Queen,
I, your passion that refuses to die.

Monsoon with Vector Anophelines

The ceiling fan turned on: full power.
The mosquito nets flutter all night.
Even the monsoon sky clears
and if the children opened their eyes now
they'd be blinded by moonlight.

But the children will not stir
and in the morning
they won't remember their dreams.

Soon, the youngest boy, who's almost two,
will burn with a fever.
This will go on for days
until he starts to sweat and then shiver
in the cold damp sheets. Then the fever
will return. This will go on for weeks.

His mother will stay by his side.
Nights she'll spend on the floor
                    by his cot
until she's certain he'll live.

But for now his mother
still sleeps on, unaware of that future
while the ceiling fan in her room
raises such a strong breeze
from the sticky moist air –
that loose strands of her hair fly wildly,
and blow across her face.

More Fears about the Moon

1

Fetus after fetus lost.

And the inner voice
dares not speak to me.

Each time I looked
there was always too much blood.
I could never see the face.
Only the fins: limp,
but they glistened and once,
the curved spine seemed to tremble
in the dish.
Too many little ones slipped away
from me. My girls,
my boys – couldn't wait
to leave – my crooked fishes
my sea horses – they didn't want
to become children.

Fetus after fetus lost.
Can't you take me away
from this city?

2

The full moon kept us
awake all night.

And in the morning
her ghost smile took us
out to the ocean,
made us walk for hours
along the edge of sand and water.

Soon we came to the place where the dolphin lay.

The dolphin lay far inland,
dead – thrown up by some great wave.

We circle it. The split open bruises,
bloated purple – the torn skin.
You cover its eyes with mussel shells.
And we walk on – but return
the next day and the next, everyday
until the tide shifts.

3

Now each day the ocean comes closer.

It crawls, it leaps, this rising tide –
while the moon shrinks.

We watch from the doorway.

What if the waves never turned back,
but kept on rising, higher and higher?
What if the moon lost control
and let the tides go as they please?

Lizard, Iguana, Chameleon, Salamander.

for Jakobine von Dömming

Who are you? The frog asks:
Lizard? Iguana? Chameleon?
Salamander?

You worry too much
about your tail.

I've gone beyond
my adolescent tadpole phase.
I've willed myself huge
        and I pray
to a huge striped fish
who is my love and my God,
green as the tree of life.

I'm the sort of frog
Frida Kahlo had in mind
when she saw Diego
as a *boy frog standing up*
on his hind legs.

Who are you, lizard?

You say the monks pray to you
but that's because
they don't know of me yet.

They walk and they walk
through blue, almost black
through red, almost black mountains
where vultures fly
over their heads –

They sing and they sing
to their water-buffalo –
guided by a crow, confused by a lizard.

I have seen the blue monk
walking with his old zebra.

What do you know, lizard?

But lizard only smiles
sly as a canoe on a lake
              at night –
Lizard sticks out her sliver of a tongue
lizard flicks her tail
and moves sudden
as an arrow –

Who am I? Lizard whispers
              Who am I?

What does it matter
as long as I can change
into any colour –
What does it matter
as long as I bring luck
to every place I visit.

Sharda

After all these years
my mother has forgotten her name –
the name of the girl
she most admired –
the girl who lived across the street
when my mother was little.

So I tell her
it must have been Sharda.
Sharda:
A mature name, full of dignity.
Sharda, who is the lute: Veena –
light sun-notes flicker
transparent across blood-dark
heavy tones – Sharda who is both
Sarasvati and Durga –
dragonfly wings
shimmer, curious above the drowned squirrel –
How can one name
contain so much?

'Sharda, Sharda!' I can see
her mother calling her.

Sharda was a serious girl.
She wore a silk *chanya choli*:
that is, a long full skirt and a tight
bodice-blouse – she sparkled.
She was nine-years-old.
She knew many prayers.
She sat alone
in the *puja* room –
she was doing *arti*
she was ringing the small brass
prayer bell with one hand
and holding a small flame
also brass cupped in her other
hand – when she slipped
and the *ghee* spilled across
her silk clothes and the wick
spit fire over her fingertips.

99

Maybe there was a gust of wind –
                something fluky
so even the huge crows fled
with their elbow-wings.

Why was there nobody
                at home that day?
Why was there no one
                who heard her cry?

'Such things happen,'
My mother says.
I suspect Sharda's elders.
Did she have too many sisters?
'No, no! It wasn't like that.'
My mother shakes her head.

Still, we can agree about how
she spun, hopping around
                and around
trying to escape the flames.

Then she was sucked in –
it was like a sudden wave
a wall
with a sharp undertow –
A fire-wave
almost silent
compared to water.

'Sharda, Sharda!'
My mother must have called
for a long time
even after they found her.

V
રિયાજ (Riyaj)

*It's for no one, it's for oneself, one writes it down,
otherwise you'd forget it. It's for yourself. You're not
leaving it for anyone else's benefit – you leave it as a snail
leaves a trace. You leave it, no more. You can't do
anything else but leave it.*

Samuel Beckett

*We all agree that your theory is crazy,
but is it crazy enough?*

Niels Bohr

રિયાજ *(riyaj), meaning practice, praxis, rehearsal, and/or
a meditative discipline, is a term used by Indian classical
musicians to describe their solitary hours with music. For
some it is an exercise in musical grammar that seeks future
completion, for others it is deeply individual and whole.*

based on Kabir Mohanty's definition

The Voices

First, a sound from an animal
you can never imagine.

Then: insect-rustle, fish-hush.

And then the voices became louder.

Voice of an angel who is newly dead.
Voice of a child who refuses
to ever become an angel with wings.

Voice of tamarinds.
Voice of the colour blue.
Voice of the colour green.
Voice of the worms.
Voice of the white roses.
Voice of the leaves torn by goats.
Voice of snake-spit.
Voice of the placenta.
Voice of the fetal heartbeat.
Voice of the scalped skull
whose hair hangs behind glass
in a museum.

I used to think there was
only one voice.
I used to wait
patiently for that one voice to return
to begin its dictation.

I was wrong.

I can never finish counting them now.
I can never finish
writing all they have to say.

Voice of the ghost who wants
to die again, but this time
in a brighter room with fragrant flowers
and different relatives.
Voice of the frozen lake.
Voice of the fog.
Voice of the air while it snows.
Voice of the girl
who still sees unicorns
and speaks to angels she knows by name.
Voice of pine tree sap.

And then the voices became louder.

Sometimes I hear them
laughing at my confusion.

And each voice insists
        and each voice knows
that it is the true one.

And each voice says: *follow me*
follow me and I will take you –

Consciousness

I am so red now
and I sparkle –
So the fuchsia sulks – jealous.

And a woman walking by
dreams a silk blouse
in my colour would suit her.

I am so red now
the children have been warned
not to touch me.

But my red silk
will lure the birds.
They'll eat me –

their beaks will tingle
their feathers tremble
as they feel my consciousness
              interrupt theirs.

Translation: Meditation on a Poem by Hasmukh Pathak

1   રાજઘાટ પર
    (Rajghat Par)

આટલાં ફૂલો નીચે ને આટલો લાંબો સમય
(aatla foolo neechay nay aatlo lambo samai)
ગાંધી કદી સૂતા નથી —
(Gandhi kadi soota nathi)
                                        – Hasmukh Pathak

2

At the Rajghat

Beneath so many flowers and for such a long time
Gandhi never sleeps –

(Dear reader, notice the present tense.)

3

Gandhi never slept for such a long time
and never slept beneath so many flowers –
And he still doesn't sleep.

4

આટલાં ફૂલો નીચે . . .   કેટલા ફૂલો નીચે ?
(aatla foolo neechay… kaitla foolo neechay?)
મનમાં જાગે છે ફૂલોની સુગંધ
(munma jaagay chay fooloni sughand)
મનમાં ઢળે છે ફૂલોનાં રંગ
(munma dhalay chay foolona rung)
મન ભૂલી પડ્યું ફૂલોમાં . . .
(mun bhooli padyu fooloma)
આટલાં ફૂલો નીચે, આટલાં ફૂલો નીચે
(aatla foolo neechay, aatla foolo neechay)
ઘૂસી ગયું મન.
(ghoosee gayu mun)

106

5

The mind refuses to forget
the scent, the colours –
The mind is lost
              between the flowers –
Beneath so many flowers, beneath so many flowers
              the mind slipped in.

6

ને આટલો લાંબો સમય . . .
(nay aatlo lambo samai)
ને કેટલો લાંબો સમય ?
(nay kaitlo lambo samai?)
સમય ક્યારે લાંબો લાગે ?
(samai kyaray lambo laagay?)

And for such a long time…
And for how long?
When does it feel like 'such a long time'?

7

ગાંધી કદી સૂતા નથી.
(Gandhi kadi soota nathi)
ગાંધી માત્ર આડા પડ્યાં હતા.
(Gandhi matra aada padya hata)
ગાંધી ઊંઘમાં પણ લખતા હતા.
(Gandhi oonghma pun lakhta hata)
પરંતુ ગાંધી કદી સૂતા નથી, કદી સૂતા નથી.
(parantu Gandhi kadi soota nathi, kadi soota nathi)

8

Gandhi never sleeps.
Gandhi was just lying down, just stretching out –
Gandhi wrote and wrote – even in his sleep
              Gandhi wrote.
But Gandhi never sleeps. He never sleeps.

9

આટલાં ફૂલો નીચે ને આટલો લાંબો સમય :
(aatla foolo neechay nay aatlo lambo samai)
નજર પડી પહેલા તો ફૂલો પર.
(najar padi pahayla to foolo par)
ફૂલો સામે જોતા જોતા
(foolo samay jota jota)
સમય યાદ આવ્યો.
(samai yad aavyo)
ગાંધી જાગતા નથી.   ગાંધી સૂતા નથી.
(Gandhi jagta nathi. Gandhi soota nathi)
આટલાં ફૂલો નીચે
(aatla foolo neechay)
          શું કરે છે ગાંધી ?
          (shoo karay chay Gandhi?)

10

Beneath so many flowers and for such a long time:
First the flowers were noticed –
they were looked at, stared at
for such a long time
so of course Time was recalled –
and then it was Time who stared at the flowers.

Gandhi will not wake up. Gandhi isn't asleep.
Beneath so many flowers
          what is Gandhi doing?

11

But he is still here –
you only have to listen,
          simply listen.

First Rain

આવ રે વરસાદ
(*aav ray varsad*)
ઘેબરીયો પરસાદ
(*ghabriyo parsad*)
ઊની ઊની રોટલી
(*oonee oonee rotli*)
ને કારેલાનું શાક
(*nay karaylanu shak*)
પહેલો વરસાદ આવે ત્યારે
(pahaylo varsad aavay tyaray –)

First rain and the earth
smells so – the soil smells
so – there is no word for it –
but this smell makes one hungry.

પહેલો વરસાદ આવે ત્યારે
(pahaylo varsad aavay tyaray)

When the first rain falls
what do you hear? What do you remember?

પવન, પંખો, વીજળી, બારી, બારણું –
(pavan, pankno, vijli, bari, barnu –)
હીંચકો –
(hinchko –)
હીંચકે બેઠાં બેઠાં જે ગીત સાંભળ્યું –
(hinchkay baytha baytha jay geet sambhalyu)

When the first rain falls
I remember my hunger.

Sruti

Sruti means 'to hear' or 'that which is heard'. Musically it points to the interval between notes which can be just perceived auditorily.

— B.C. Deva

You, who first said *sruti*,
what did you hear?

Between the sound of your footsteps
and the cry of a bird by the river
did you hear another?
Did you continue walking?

Where did you turn
to measure your scale?

Between the sound of a horse
stepping forward: his bare skin quivering, his head raised,
and the sound of a woman
buying rice, didn't you hear another
and yet another sound?

What did you listen for
to count your notes?

You, who first said *sruti*,
you keep me sleepless.
I'm trying to find a way
to return to the world that you once heard.

Water

for Phyllis Webb

જળ અથવા પાણી
(jal athva pani)
પાણી અથવા જળ
(pani athva jal)

This word for water or that word for water –

A broken song?
Or the inner poet
searching for the right word?
The inner eye
the inner ear

wanting જળ (jal) and પાણી (pani) –
      to rush through water
જળ (jal) પાણી (pani) water
All these words bleeding into each other
      like watercolours.

આપણે તુલસીના ક્યારામાં જળ સીંચયે
(aapnay tulsina kyarama jal seenchyay)
ગુલાબના ક્યારામાં પાણી રેડીયે
(gulabna kyarama pani radeyay)
અને પ્યાલામાં તો હમેશા પાણી ભરાય
(anay pyalama tow hamaisha pani bharai)
જળ અથવા પાણી
(jal athva pani)

chants the pure voice
that dictates me,
the 'I' who is now tape-recorder.

જળ અથવા પાણી
(jal athva pani) comes unbidden
uncontrollable as rain.
જળ અથવા પાણી
(jal athva pani)

111

A child's game?
My very own fragments from Ahmedabad?

જળ અથવા પાણી
(jal athva pani)
will I accept this
without further meaning, without pictures,
without a little story?

What do I mean

જળ અથવા પાણી
(jal athva pani)

Nuances of water –

જળ સીંચવું
(jal seenchvu)

પાણી રેડવું
(pani radevu)

What is the true sound of water?

Sitar, jaltarang, the inner voice speaks:
જળ, જળ, જળ
(jal, jal, jal)

The inner voice,
that bright spirit who nags and teases
can speak sitar sounds
while the human tongue
is too thick and clumsy
inside the human mouth.

Frauenjournal

A woman kills
her newborn granddaughter
because she has four already.

A woman kills because
there's not enough money
not enough milk.

A woman kills her newborn daughter
and still eats dinner
and still wears a green sari.

Is this being judgemental?
Or is this how one bears witness
            with words?

And another woman in another country
makes sure that her seven-year-old daughter
has her clitoris sliced off
with a razor blade.
This is what they will show us
tonight – prime time –
We're advised not to let our children watch this.
This has never been filmed before.
Sometimes it's necessary
to see the truth. The moderator tells us
words are not enough.

Now the camera focuses on
the razor blade – so there is no doubt
about the instrument. The razor blade
            is not a rumour.

Now the camera shifts over
to the seven-year-old face:
she smiles – innocent – she doesn't know.
The girl smiles – she feels important.
And then the blood and then the screams.

Why do I think I have to watch this?
Is this being a voyeur?
Or is this how one begins
to bear witness?

And another woman tells us how years ago
she accidentally killed her own daughter
while trying to cut out her clitoris.
The risks are great, she tells us,
but she's proud of her profession.

How much reality can you bear?

And if you are a true poet
why can't you cure
       anything with your words?

The camera focused
long and steady on the razor blade.
At least it wasn't rusty.

How can you bear witness
with words, how can you heal
       anything with words?

The camerawoman could not
afford to tremble or flinch.
She had to keep a steady hand.
And the hand holding the razor blade
did not hesitate.

And if you are a true poet
will you also find a voice
for the woman who can smile
after killing her daughter?

What is the point of bearing witness?

Afterwards, the girl can barely walk.

For days the girl will hobble – unable

unable unable

unable to return
to her old self,
her old childish way of life.

114

Notes

p. 24   'Cow's Skull – Red, White and Blue': This poem refers to Georgia O'Keeffe's painting, *Cow's Skull – Red, White and Blue*, 1931.

p. 25   'Skinnydipping in History': All parts in italics are quotations from John Ashbery's poems.

p. 35   'Pelvis with Moon': This poem is a response to Georgia O'Keeffe's painting, *Pelvis with Moon*, 1943.

p. 41   'Ninniku': When Buddhism came to Japan in the sixth century AD the Japanese adopted a new word for garlic, *ninniku*, the characters for which mean 'to bear insults with patience'. Buddhist monks are permitted to use garlic for its medicinal properties. The Japanese have never been enthusiastic garlic-eaters. This information from: Stephen Fulder and John Blackwood, *Garlic: Nature's Original Remedy* (Healing Arts Press, Vermont, USA) 1991.

p. 46   'Mars Owns this Herb': The title of this poem is a quotation from *Culpeper's Complete Herbal*.

p. 48   'Bear's Garlic at Nevern': Sheila na Gig is the Welsh fertility goddess. *Devi* is the Sanskrit word for goddess.

p. 65   'The Good Farmer': *Knoblauch* is the German word for garlic.

p. 69   'Garlic and Sapphires in the Mud': The title of this poem is a line from T.S. Eliot's *Four Quartets*.

p. 76   'A Gujarati Patient Speaks': The epigraph is a quotation from Otto Friedrich, *Glenn Gould: A Life and Variations* (Lester & Orpen Dennys Ltd, Toronto, Canada) 1989.

p. 91   'Paula Modersohn-Becker Speaks to Herself': This poem refers to Paula Modersohn-Becker's painting, *Selbstbildnis am 6. Hochzeitstag*, 1906.

p. 95   'More Fears about the Moon': This poem partly addresses itself to a poem by Eleanor Wilner, 'Fears about the Moon', in her book *Otherwise* (University of Chicago Press) 1993.

p. 97   'Lizard, Iguana, Chameleon, Salamander': This poem is a response to a series of paintings by Jakobine von Dömming.